Blackpool

IN OLD PHOTOGRAPHS

The Helter Skelter Slide, South Shore, in the early 1900s, with Sir Hiram Maxim's Captive Flying Machine.

Blackpool

IN OLD PHOTOGRAPHS

CATHERINE ROTHWELL

Alan Sutton Publishing Limited
Phoenix Mill · Far Thrupp · Stroud
Gloucestershire

First Published 1994

Copyright © Catherine Rothwell, 1994

British Library Cataloguing in Publication Data.
A catalogue record for this book is available from
the British Library.

ISBN 0-7509-0810-6

Typeset in 9/10 Sabon.
Typesetting and origination by
Alan Sutton Publishing Limited.
Printed in Great Britain by
Ebenezer Baylis, Worcester.

Contents

The wrought-iron drinking fountain, Talbot Square, 1880.

Introduction

There can be no better example of Victorian enterprise than the amazing success story of Blackpool whose pioneering spirit embodied all the unflagging, indomitable confidence of that age. 'He who dares – wins.' This was the watchword, and bold publicity coupled with diligent application of the town's motto 'Progress' proved it to be true.

Perhaps the most electrifying of Blackpool's men of the moment was Dr William Henry Cocker, for four years Chairman of the Local Board, Charter Mayor in 1876 and mayor on five later occasions. Within a few short years his lavish approach made Blackpool a nationwide talking point.

When the Winter Gardens opened, the civic heads of fifty cities and boroughs plus the Lord Mayor of London with all his sheriffs were guests of Dr Cocker for a week at the Imperial Hydro. No one ever knew what this bill of legendary proportions came to, but the urbane doctor unflinchingly settled the account. With such strokes of advertising genius, although he finally impoverished himself, his beloved town rose above all other resorts. His contemporaries whirled alongside, fired by his ambitions: 'a restless spirit', 'a man of fascinating magnetism', 'he could peer into the future'. Dr Cocker was followed by the Bickerstaffe brothers, W.G. Bean and other people of stature – talented council members and the Thompson family – all contributing to the large-scale construction which became Blackpool's hallmark from the Tower downwards.

Wonderful air blew across the Irish Sea (the founding fathers not only exploited its turbulent moods, they fought it fearlessly with strong sea defences). There were great natural advantages: 7 miles of flat, golden sands washed twice daily by no ordinary sea but 'the bounding main'. With the help of the railways, equally confident and zealous, the workers were speedily brought from sprawling, industrial areas and once in, they were captivated. Here was splendour in buildings and interiors envisaged only in fairy tales. Here was safe bathing (all the rage) and the facilities that went with it. Here was a cornucopia of entertainment and daylong merriment extending into night. Here was quality at an unbelievably reasonable price and, above all, here was that wonder – the Tower.

Registered on 19 February 1891, the Blackpool Tower Company Ltd went on to save £21,200 in a deal with the London-based Standard Contract & Debenture Corporation. John Bickerstaffe, blessed with northern grit and prescience, routed the London capitalists and by September the Tower's foundation stone was well and truly laid. Local memories recall muscular navvies who dug out the foundations with picks and shovels and the sumptuous banquet that followed Sir Matthew White-Ridley's visit: a display of silver candelabra and a long menu including grouse, calf's head, haunch of venison and Pudding à la Eiffel.

Every Bank Holiday after the opening of Blackpool Tower signalled some new and entrancing addition to the pleasure dromes. The crowds came in their thousands year after year, as children, with their own children, and with their grandchildren, to 'wonderful Blackpool, the most progressive resort under the flag'. When the first pile of the North Pier was screwed into the clay on 27 June 1862 Major Francis Preston, Chairman of the North Pier Company, prophesied that 'it would grow into one of the most amazing aggregations of public amusement in the world'. Another pioneer was to be proved correct.

On that red-letter day when the North Pier opened trains chuffed into Blackpool since dawn from all over the country. Fun-loving spirit overflowed, as did the inns and ale houses. Flags and bunting fluttered in the salty air while daredevils threatened to dive off the end of the pier; some did. Aquatics were to become a speciality, the Irish Sea deciding some of the principal swimming championships in the world.

For spectacular entertainment presented in grand and often rip-roaring style, Blackpool had no serious rival other than America's Coney Island, but Blackpool also offered culture. In those glittering years before fire destroyed the Indian Pavilion, some of the greatest instrumental and vocal artistes in the world played before Blackpool audiences. Going one better seemed to be in the genes of the townspeople. Ridgeways, pork butchers of Central Drive who had the best reputation for Lancashire cheese, claimed that their Blackpool puddings – 'fresh and hot every afternoon', a matter of no small importance – were better than Bury puddings. Annually, unassailable Blackpool girded up its loins for the race it has never stopped running.

Today's crowds thronging the piers, the promenade or the Golden Mile, some clutching candyfloss in one hand and a 'Kiss Me Quick' hat in the other, can look forward, as ever, to the greatest free show on earth: Blackpool Illuminations – 5 miles of animated tableaux and fairy lights. Where else?

That bright and breezy, free and easy atmosphere is still at large in 1994, the centenary year of Blackpool Tower, which not only welcomes Her Majesty the Queen but rejoices in The Big One, the highest and fastest roller coaster in the world.

The story of how a remote fishing village became a world-famous resort of glittering amusement and novelty is told here in old photographs.

SECTION ONE

A Remote Fishing Village

Carlton Terrace, North Shore, 1867.

An eighteenth-century print of what became Blackpool's Talbot Square as far as Church Street. When William Hutton came in 1788 he wrote: 'Houses are scattered along the seabank for a mile. There is no place of worship.' 'Blackpool was named from a peaty brook long ago,' reported *Round the Coast* in 1902, 'but now its fine sands make it one of the best bathing places.' When early building started relics were discovered in deposits of peat: two stone hand mills, an antique cheese vat, a dagger, nails, a brass axe, a few silver coins and a groat dating from the reign of Henry IV. The Revd W. Thornber, the first vicar of Blackpool (see p.32), possessed a blue marble monumental fragment engraved with an urn. He also found an iron palstave inland from here in the Great Carleton area. Before the interest of visitors was aroused by the sudden mania for sea water, occupants of this coastal area fished and farmed for a living.

In the eighteenth century the site of Blackpool was a waste of marram-covered sandhills beyond the few mud huts of the fishing village. Adjoining stretches of moss and marshland led to Marton Mere from where a peat-blackened stream flowed into the sea – hence Black Pull or Pool.

Hygiene Terrace with the Beach and Royal hotels, late 1840s. An early *Guide to Blackpool* refers to 'scores of excellent hotels. Some of architectural pretensions that deserve specific notice are studded here and there on the front. The hotels are of a high order and are conducted on a liberal scale.'

Fox Hall or Vauxhall in the eighteenth century was the hunting lodge of the Tyldesley family of Myerscough. Declared a freehold house in 1717 when Agatha Tyldesley, widow, registered her estate; by 1865 it was the Foxhall Hotel. The ancient barn with the Tyldesley coat of arms in one wall remained but the armorial bearings were claimed by a Liverpool family.

Central Beach, with the Albion and Lane Ends hotels and a paddle-steamer, 1840s. Blackpool's first steamer of this kind to be introduced was the *Wellington*. In 1880 another hotel proprietor George Seed had one of the first telephones: no. 7.

Photographed in 1898, eighteen years after the epic rescue of the schooner, *Bessie Jones*, laden with steel rails, these lifeboatmen are survivors of the crew that went to the rescue in lifeboat *Robert William* on 26 February 1880. Left to right: J. Smith, J. Wylie, J. Fish, Bob Bickerstaffe, W. Owen, Richard Parr, James Stanhope. Four lives were saved but unfortunately one was lost. Because of high seas and extreme cold it was an enormous task. In a north-westerly gale amid showers of hail Bob Bickerstaffe took charge as coxswain; Jack Parkinson, bowman, and Messrs Swarbrick and Rimmer were also in the lifeboat. At that time the houses in Tyldesley Terrace were only half built and a watching crowd sheltered there while Mr Cunliffe and Mr Irving took charge of the lifeboat cart and the restive horses. The crew of the *Bessie Jones* had taken refuge in the rigging. It took two hours to effect this most difficult rescue.

The Gynn Inn, high on the cliffs, around the turn of the century, where stories of smuggling and sea wrecks must have been exchanged over the pewter pots. In 1833, guided by a lighted candle at the Gynn, a Scottish sloop was saved. In 1850 the brig *Portia* came ashore in a storm near Uncle Tom's Cabin (see p. 66).

Regent's Terrace and Brighton Parade, 1867. A decorous Victorian scene with the Parish Church on the right, but as early as 1852 some newspapers denounced 'Blackpool's rowdy Sundays'. In February of that year Blackpool's shops were lit by gas for the first time, a water spout was seen offshore and at Christmas a hurricane played havoc, sinking pleasure boats and fishing smacks.

The beach at Blackpool, 1840. The famous water-colourist David Cox, born in 1783, visited Blackpool with fellow-painter William Roberts but 'found little worth painting'. Of the two sketches showing the sea front and lodgings where they stayed, one was presented to Mrs Roberts. Cox's painting shows the unmade esplanade and shallow cliffs sloping to the sea, with the 'Northern Mountains' in the distance. The Royal Hotel is on the far right. (Courtesy Courtauld Gallery.)

Blackpool Old Road in the nineteenth century, the route taken regularly by farmers and early landladies on horseback or with pony and cart to buy supplies from the market town of Poulton. One enterprising native brought sweet water from here to sell to visitors in Blackpool.

An engraving from the *Illustrated London News*, September 1856. Originally a hamlet in the township of Layton-cum-Warbreck in Bispham parish, 'New Blackpool' began to attract visitors in 1745. By 1836 the parish was divided into three districts, Blackpool's boundaries being Bridge House Lane, Whinney Heys, Great Layton and Boonley as far as the Gynn Inn.

The Carlin Stone at Norbreck, 1909. Together with Pennystone (so called because pennies were left on the stone for jugs of ale), they were once part of Blackpool's shore. In the sixteenth century villagers fled as the sea submerged their hamlet. Likewise Singleton Thorpe vanished, villagers setting up homes inland at Singleton. The site of Pennystone was investigated by the Blackpool Ramblers Association in 1922 and evidence of a settlement (tree trunks, door lintels) was found.

Rossall Farm, Hawes Side Lane, opposite the old Highfield Hotel, 1900. The lamp on the corner of Highfield Road was lit by sewer gas. Richard F. Rossall, born in 1860, was the son of Thomas and Alice Rossall who were strict Baptists. At that time Layton Hawes was owned by the Lord of the Manor, Peter Hesketh Fleetwood.

The interior of the first Church of St Paul, Marton, erected by public subscription and opened by licence in 1804, seen here in the 1890s. The old church was lengthened, a tower added and a porch erected in 1848. Previously oil lamps were used. George Garsden, a licensee who died in 1869, and Mrs Walsh who died in 1793, the great-great-grandmother of a Marton resident, were both buried here.

A thatched cruck cottage and sea-pebble wall in Lee Road, Marton, in the nineteenth century. Mr J. Ball, who lived there and died in 1919, grew fruit trees in an area later covered with acres of glass greenhouses. These traditional Fylde cottages were supported at the gable end by split, forked tree trunks.

The Star Inn, 1880, where visitors bought tea, coffee or Dublin Stout before visiting the gypsy encampment. The sign read: 'Gypsy Sarah's only clever daughter-in-law – the clever seeing lady Jennie Boswell, patronised by His Majesty'. Placed above the flimsy tents and jaunty, carved gypsy caravans, these substantial wooden boards pulled in the crowds.

The crew of the *Robert William* with the members of the lifeboat committee standing below, 1864. In the lifeboat, left to right: Bob Bickerstaffe, John Swarbrick, Tom Maudsley, Tom Fish (seated), S. Jolly (standing with his hand on his brother's shoulder), W. Jolly (seated), Sam Rimmer, Jim Parr (seated), Jack Parkinson, Richard Gaskell, James Swarbrick, James Stanhope, William Parr. By this time, the population of Blackpool had risen to 3,500.

A painting by Washington Hotel innkeeper, George Barrett, of the *Robert William* going out to rescue the *Bessie Jones*, 1880. Such a rescue, in one of the fiercest storms ever experienced in Blackpool, won each crew member a special silver medal in the shape of a cross, plus a few pounds in money.

A shooting party, *c*. 1870. Throughout the Fylde it was acknowledged that 'custom granted to all the use of the gun at Christmas'. Hare shooting, as apart from hare coursing, was usually organized, but conies (the old name for rabbits) were kept under control by the warrener or gamekeeper. 'Cymbling' for larks, 'snigging' for eels, and hunting rabbits and hares and even larger animals was a means of supplementing diet, but taking game was illegal as it belonged to the landowners who employed gamekeepers to prevent poaching. On 'shoot' days farm workers and villagers were employed as beaters. As Fox Hall was built originally as a hunting lodge for the Tyldesleys, Blackpool must have offered some good sport.

Rustic Cottage, 1900. Norbreck's oldest cottage, dating from the seventeenth century, was home to the Wilson family. Captain James Preston who lived opposite bought the cottage, eventually selling it to Norbreck Hydro. Of typical vernacular architecture, driftwood from the beach formed the gatepost canopy and the low cobbled wall was built from pebbles. Rustic Cottage was demolished in 1924.

The cart road on the front at Blackpool, 1840s. The beach already has a bathing machine. Horse riding and promenading, recommended by the medical profession, are evident. In the eighteenth century it was recorded that sufficient space for three cart roads was left when building, but all were lost as the cliffs wore down.

Mr Swarbrick, a Norbreck fisherman, preparing rods and lines, *c.* 1860. Nine boats were then catching haddock and cod of which 12 cwt were sold weekly on Preston market. Baulks were set up at South Shore and large quantities of fish caught. The arrival of steam vessels and the removal of 'gnarrs' or banks of encrusted stone drove the fish away to better spawning grounds.

Bispham old village, 1892. Ivy Cottage, home of the Tinkler family in 1686, is on the right. Blackpool visitors came to the tea-rooms here, the picturesque village being quite a draw. Bispham was absorbed by Blackpool in 1917. One of Bispham's characters was known as 'Owd [Old] England'. The expression 'old earth' was often applied to ancient meadowland.

The stocks, whipping post and market cross of the medieval market town of Poulton, four miles from Blackpool, *c.* 1880. Early visitors came to the old tithe barn where plays and melodramas were staged. Tickets could be bought at the Georgian inn, The Golden Ball, opposite. On the right is M. Lawrenson's shop, printer and bookseller. Stone setts have replaced even older seashore cobbles in the Square.

Bank Hey Street with the corner of Victoria Street, 1875. On the wall of the shop with its primitive sacking blind, a sign directs to the fire brigade station. Lewis's department store was built on the left. Mr Stirzaker, haircutter and perfumer, was in Bank Hey Street, and at Bank Hey House was Holt's Ladies' and Children's Outfitters.

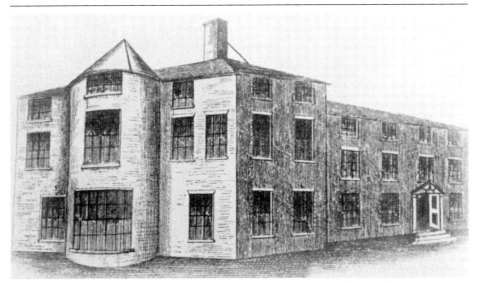

Baileys Hotel, one of the first along with Bennett's and Yorkshire House to accommodate visitors, *c.* 1770. Butcher's and Welsh's Row were early guest-cottages formed from clay plastered upon wattles (Ann Butcher was said to have purchased the first tea kettle in Blackpool for her lodgers). The site of Thomas Nickson's cottage was later occupied by the Albion Hotel. 'Old Marjory's' cottage became Bonny's Hotel.

William Fisher's farm and Fisher's cottage, Little Bispham, which dated from the seventeenth century. Apart from the farms of George Hull, William Bamber, Henry Davy, William Hull, Thomas Gaskell, John Whiteside and Thomas Shaw (who was isolated at Angersholme), there were few other dwellings.

The North Pier, when it first opened in 1868. Claimed to be the finest marine parade in Europe, 12,000 tons of metal went into its construction. The town crier's announcements greeted thousands of trippers as they spilled off Lancashire & Yorkshire Railway trains specially run for the occasion.

Norbreck House, The Castle and Barnfield (home of Captain Preston), and other buildings, 1910. These were the nucleus of Norbreck Hydro, which expanded greatly over the years. Outside this older part can still be found a sundial formed from an ice-age erratic boulder washed from the cliffs.

Whinney Heys, Blackpool, *c.* 1870. The name derived from yellow gorse or 'whin', and the house became the site of Victoria Hospital. The first house was built by James Massey of Carleton in Elizabeth I's reign. The Veale family lived there in the eighteenth century when Squire Thomas Tyldesley was a visitor.

Blackpool Central Beach in 1880, the days when swimmers had to undress in a bathing machine. J. Wolfe and R. Penswick were among the machine proprietors. Jones's Sewing Machines, Pears' Soap and other commodities or premises were advertised on the roofs and sides of these lumbering boxes on wheels.

'Shrimps alive', a postcard sent in 1905 from South Shore, Blackpool, was testimony to the visitors' love of sea food while on holiday. Certain cottages were known for selling freshly boiled shrimps daily. There were stalls on Central Beach that sold them in penny bags, but supplies were dwindling by the 1920s. Herrings, once plentiful, all disappeared and local fishermen described the sea off Blackpool as 'barren'. Tides were receding at Southport from where fishermen had emigrated to Fleetwood to continue their calling. Some Blackpool fishermen did likewise but most adapted to the new way of life – pleasing the visitors, which meant turning boatmen for pleasure trips or opening up their cottages as accommodation. Visitors in the early days came on horseback, by stagecoach or in farm carts from places as far away as Padiham, with supplies of water slung from the cart axles. Some walked all the way, but once the branch line opened from Preston to Blackpool in 1847, the railway carried droves of visitors who almost entirely deserted Fleetwood, which had a rail link from 1840.

Dr William Henry Cocker, in mayoral robes and civic chain, was one of Blackpool's founding fathers. On Easter Monday 1870 he was present at the opening ceremony of Blackpool's new promenade. In March of that year he laid the foundation stone for the new drinking fountain in Talbot Square. In 1874 he established the Aquarium which later became part of Blackpool Tower, and the following year sold his house 'Bank Hey' to the Winter Gardens Company. In 1876, the year Blackpool received its Charter of Incorporation and became a borough, Dr Cocker was elected the first mayor. He died in 1911.

Robert Bickerstaffe or Bob, as he was affectionately known in Blackpool, was the lifeboat coxswain for many years as well as Central Pier manager. His knowledge of the sea and sandbanks proved invaluable when the pier was being built. One of the oldest inhabitants, he knew the Revd W. Thornber personally. Bob was born on 4 August 1831 in a whitewashed cottage opposite the site of Central Pier. As a boy, his family apprenticed him to a Blackburn draper but he disliked it so much he ran away, returning via Marton in a carrier's cart. His uncle 'Old Bob', who was a pleasure boatman in the summer and a fisherman in winter, taught him to make boats, mend lifebuoys, fretwork, carving and plying the needle for sail making. Bob married Margaret Hull of Poulton. He died in 1913.

The family grocer of Hound Hill, Mr J. Park and his family, outside their premises in 1860. This shop became the site of Bannister's Bazaar. In the twentieth century the area was turned into the busy Hound's Hill Shopping Centre.

The 667-ton Norwegian barque *Sirene*, bound from Fleetwood for Florida, was driven before a hurricane in 1892, but fortunately had a happy landing which obviated the need for a lifeboat launch. Helpless in a terrible sea, *Sirene* headed straight for North Pier and onlookers feared a crash. Miraculously it came to a halt by the pier entrance and the promenade, so close that the crew of eleven could be hauled ashore by lifeboatmen. Two masts fell, destroying four shops at the pier entrance. Under the sea's battering the *Sirene* became a total wreck and was auctioned, broken up and carted away. Visitors loved the occasion, collecting all manner of souvenirs conveniently placed for them under the pier. Costume jewellery, furs, trinkets and so on from the wrecked shops quickly found homes all over Lancashire, increasing Blackpool's fame as a jolly good place to stay.

Carleton's Castle Gardens Hotel, *c.* 1900. In early days it was known as the Weld Arms, and was a favourite wagonette trip from Blackpool. The wrought-iron arch led through a turnstile into luxurious strawberry gardens, a bowling green, a monkey house and an orchid conservatory. On the right is the old Refreshment Room where non-alcoholic drinks were served; on the left, the wall of the village school.

Norbreck, *c.* 1900. The village presented a rural atmosphere, as did Bispham with its white cottages and thatched roofs. Norsemen coming ashore by way of Ireland and the Isle of Man resulted in Norse names like Warbreck, Norbreck and Angersholme. A mass of human bones discovered at Anchorsholme in the nineteenth century lends credence to the traditional story that a battle was fought there.

St John's Vicarage, Church Street, 1875. It was the home of the Revd W. Thornber, the first vicar of Blackpool, who became notable for fiery sermons. He worked hard to get a lifeboat for the town and made a glossary of old Fylde words, for example kibble (stick), alicar (vinegar) and ginn (road to the sea). The house became the site of the Winter Gardens.

Baines Endowed Schools, Marton, 1833. This was one of three charity schools set up under the will of James Baines, the prosperous eighteenth-century woollen dealer. The other schools, also in the Fylde, were at Thornton and Poulton.

The cliffs at North Shore still presented a wild, unspoilt appearance at the turn of the century. Since then tons of concrete have shored them up and the work still continues. The council had to stop the removal of gravel and rocks from the shore as this increased erosion.

Queen of the North, 1909. Along with other steamers it made daily sailings from North and Central piers to Douglas, Menai Bridge, Llandudno, Southport and Morecambe. The popular pleasure steamers from Blackpool had remarkably cheap fares. Blackpool Steamboat Company was established in December 1894.

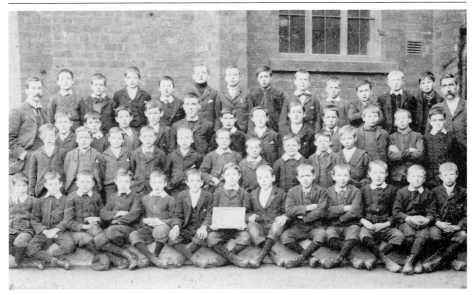

Christ Church School, *c.* 1902. The school was situated across from Talbot Road next to what became Coar's chip shop, the most popular in Blackpool. The boy sixth from the right in the front row is James Yates who became a signal and points repairer on the Lancashire & Yorkshire Railway. Standard 7 had forty-seven boys.

'Gipsy Sarah's Only Daughter in England', 1902. Many postcards were produced about these colourful characters who settled on South Beach until ejected in 1910. This one is entitled 'Gipsy Life at Blackpool'. The dynasty continues today with Leah Petulengro and her daughter Sarah on the Golden Mile and North Pier respectively.

Bispham Smithy and thatched cottages, *c*. 1942. The wheelwright's shop was next to the blacksmith's premises where ploughboys came to sharpen the coulter or cutting blade of the plough. Sea-pebble walls and cobbled areas were still there in the 1950s but all are gone now.

The seventeenth-century barn at Bamber's Farm on Red Bank Road, 1951. In the early nineteenth century George Hull farmed at Haddle House. In the area of Little Bispham with Norbreck, William Bamber, William Fisher and Henry Davy were farmers, while William Brodbelt was miller at the long-since-vanished Norbreck windmill situated on the cliffs.

Paddling, *c.* 1900. In the late nineteenth and early twentieth century firms made extensive use of bathing machines for advertisements. Lewis's advertised their 30s suits for men and in large white letters commanded: 'Wear Lewis's hats.' And people did! Even children going down to the sea for a paddle wore hats, caps or bonnets. Singleton's bathing machines advertised Dolly Blue for the whitest of washes and also advised: 'Eat the best of all breads – Hovis.' About this time Blackpool's first Musical Festival was held and promenade widening commenced which went on until May 1911. In connection with this work the 'Sands Express' was seen chugging along the front, trucks pulled on rails by the steam locomotive *Reliance* in a cloud of steam.

The Briggs family, Sam and Maggie with daughter Lillian, were photographed in the 1900s at Eddison Studios, 14 Manchester Terrace, Blackpool. The resort was very popular with workers from the shoe and slipper factories of the Rossendale valley. The all-in price of 2*s* 6*d* included a return railway ticket, admission to the Palace for music hall or dancing and a meal.

Sarah Boswell, known as Gypsy Sarah, aged 99, with her granddaughter early this century. Visitors came to her primitive tent in the sandhills near the Star Inn because she claimed to have second sight. Another Romany, Gypsy Smith, became Petulengro of the twentieth century.

Talbot Square, showing the wrought-iron drinking fountain from where horse-drawn carriages set off and locals gathered to talk, 1895. The Theatre Royal and Free Library were then functioning and Smith's Boot Store (left) had opened for business.

The promenade showing Central Pier, previously called South Pier, with small sailing yachts and rowing boats available for hire, 1895. A milk float and three landaus constitute the only traffic but crowds parade on pier and pathway, driven there by the approach of the tide. Close to North Pier was the 'best Natural Bathing Ground on the coast, an isolated portion reserved for Ladies'.

SECTION TWO

The Transformation

South Beach, 1890.

The Water Shows at the Prince of Wales Baths in the 1880s were declared 'the sight of Blackpool . . . the most amusing and side-splitting Aquatic Derby. These grand swimming entertainments will be given by the beautiful Sisters Johnson, champion swimmers of the world; Miss Hermione, the greatest scientific and ornamental lady swimmer in the world; Miss Lottie Scott, the floating wonder; Professor J.J. Collier, the champion swimmer of the world.' Professors Scott, Ross, Dutton and Parsons assisted and the Ivies Troupe brought the house down with a laughable sketch called 'The Un-Pacific Island'. Admission charges were 6*d*, 1*s* and 2*s*.

The Aquarium, Aviary and Menagerie formed by William H. Cocker opened in 1875. This early attempt to please visitors was purchased by the Blackpool Tower Company whose first chairman was Alderman John Bickerstaffe. On this site the foundation stone of the Tower was laid on 25 September 1891 by the Blackpool MP, Sir Matthew White-Ridley.

The building of Blackpool Tower, 1893. By 10 April the metal construction had reached 168 ft. The Aquarium, Aviary and Menagerie, later incorporated into the main building, functioned alongside. Entry through the turnstiles to see the fishes and animals cost 6d. Grateful shareholders rewarded Alderman John Bickerstaffe with a 4 ft silver model of the Tower for his enterprise. In later years John also received a massive silver salver and was made a Freeman of the Borough for his role in an amazingly successful venture that never looked back.

A tricycle on the promenade has the road almost to itself, with landaus ahead and Blackpool Tower rising, c. 1892. The electric street tramway on the left, opened 29 September 1885, was designed by Holroyd Smith.

This Blackpool gentleman from 1870, name unknown, could have been associated with the great ventures that earned the town its reputation for innovation: the electricity works opened by Lord Kelvin in 1893, the police courts built in South King Street in 1892 at a cost of £20,560, the fire brigade station costing £9,288 erected in 1906, the Blackpool and Fleetwood Tramroad opened on 13 July 1898, or possibly the Fylde Water Board. At the height of the season when the town was crammed with visitors the question of water supply was pressing, until the inauguration in July 1932 by Prince George of the Hodder Water Supply. Members of the board had many anxious hours in the 1890s when the first reservoirs were completed, as rapid growth in resident population and visitor influx made it clear that existing provision was inadequate.

Sisters from Fleetwood, photographed in Ash Martin's Studio in Adelaide Street, who visited Blackpool for the ladies' fashion shops: Goulden's of Church Street, Grimshaw's of Leopold Grove opposite St John's Church, Riley & Sons of Lytham Street or Critchley's, the linen house, which had three shops in the town. Whole departments were given up to trimmings: ribbons, lace, swansdown, fur tippets and jumper silk, the latter 5s 11d per hank. The sisters are wearing gowns with the then fashionable leg-of-mutton sleeves, and one is thought to be Ada Constance Agnes Barnes, born 25 May 1899.

Blackpool's North Pier, seen here in 1890, was without rival in the country. Whit Monday crowds featured bonnets, flower-strewn Edwardian hats, nautical caps, straw boaters and flat Lancashire caps. The press of humanity was so great one wonders at the enjoyment but it proved the point: 'Blackpool will not be left behind in any respect.' The kiosk on the left advertised the Torpedo Washer Company; opposite was a fancy bazaar, but at the end of the pier on the right was the greatest attraction: the Indian Pavilion. Crowds poured in to view this spellbinding authentic building based on the Temple of Bunderaband in India. Nightly concerts before two thousand people were given by the world's greatest instrumentalists and singers, including Signor Foli and Madame Trebelli. Professor Simon Speelman of the Hallé Orchestra and Sir Charles and Lady Hallé increased its fame. A disastrous fire in 1921 totally destroyed the Pavilion; the sale of salvage raised £310.

Laying the foundation stone for the police courts when Henry Buckley was mayor, 1892. The borough police force was formed on 1 July 1887 and comprised Chief Constable Mr C.J. Denham, one inspector, three sergeants and eighteen constables. As the fishing village transformed itself into the Wonderland of the World, foundation stone laying became a feature and much was made of each occasion as Blackpool, from the early days, thrived on publicity. Throughout the 1870s every year was marked with some major event furthering the town's progress. Not least was John Grime's publication of the *Blackpool Gazette* and the appearance four years later of the *Blackpool Times*. Backed by the dynamic Mr Naden's publicity department for the borough, the Victorian years at Blackpool were a success story unique in Britain.

The ship's bell of the *Abana*, the 256-ton New Brunswick barque bound for Savannah, wrecked in December 1894 on a night when there was a great frost with ice floes in the sea. When it grounded near the clay cliffs of Norbreck, the *Abana's* sails were in ribbons and the mainmast was gone. Sailing the lifeboat up the coast in the storm was impossible, so it was dragged by horses via country lanes through Bispham. Although only 400 yd from shore, the crew of the *Abana* gave up hope, waiting two hours until the *Robert William* was launched from the beach. All seventeen crew were resuscitated at the Red Lion. The ship's bell was given to Mr Hindle, the innkeeper, who raised the alarm. It is now kept at St Andrew's Church, Cleveleys.

Blackpool Town Hall in 1900, the year when Thomas Houldsworth Smith was mayor. The Town Hall cost £815,000, the Council Chamber being magnificently appointed. The premises of Wright's confectioners, and J.S. Todd, silk merchants, were swept away, as was the wrought-iron drinking fountain, a favourite meeting place in early days but in the way when the tram track was laid.

Talbot Square, 1860. The Church of the Sacred Heart, Pugin's beautiful Gothic structure, was erected in 1857. Street lighting had arrived as evidenced by the lamp (the Improvement Act covering gas and the market was passed in 1853), but the area is as yet relatively undeveloped.

In the early years of Wakes Weeks, when entire Lancashire towns closed down and came to Blackpool, c. 1880. The six girls, probably from cotton mills, are seated side-saddle and have lined up for the beach photographer with the donkey man on the right. Blackpool Billposting Company, in the background, was founded in the early years.

The Roman Catholic Church of the Sacred Heart, one of Blackpool's fine early buildings, 1900. Standing opposite the entrance to North Pier in Talbot Road, the church tower was referred to as 'a fine example of the vigorous treatment by a modern architect of beautiful Decorative style. . . . The large lantern where the transept intersects the main body of the church effectively breaks the roof line.' Architect A.W.N. Pugin, a convert to Roman Catholicism, designed many RC churches and was much in demand during the Victorian era. For Blackpool, only the acknowledged best would do. Miss Tempest of Broughton Hall, Yorkshire, paid for the erection of the church of which the Revd Charles Widdowson and Henry Shea were pastors.

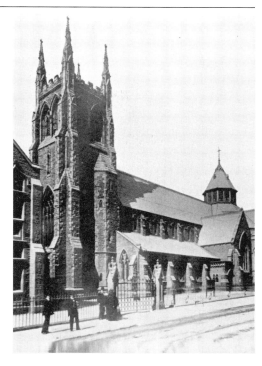

The old windmill at Great Marton was pulled down in 1900. It stood next to the Oxford Hotel where J. Gorse was licensee. Five storeys high and constructed of bricks, it resembled Staining mill, having a similar 'cap' which was shaped like an upturned boat. Thomas Moore, who was miller in around 1820, was involved in the development of South Shore in the nineteenth century.

Blackpool Free Public Library and Reading Room was officially opened by the Earl of Derby on 16 June 1880; it was open daily from 9 a.m. to 10 p.m. Miss Hannah Eteson was the first librarian and Kate Lewtas and Bertha Barrow were assistants. This building was the old Assembly Rooms.

The Theatre Royal in Talbot Square, which formed a portion of the Arcade and Assembly Rooms, 1870. Its great rival was the Prince of Wales Theatre on the promenade in a block of buildings then known as the Lane Ends Estate.

This young lady was photographed in about 1900 by Fred Ash of South Beach, who specialized in cabinet portraits for visitors. Besides studios in Bolton and Manchester he also had premises at South Beach, 41A Church Street and Regent Square ('opposite the New Promenade North Shore'). The population had then swelled to 52,860, not counting visitors. By 1933 it had risen to 101,543.

Sarah Fielding of Rossendale, related to the Fieldings of Knowle Farm, was a visitor to the old Aquarium and Menagerie. She accompanied Ethel Fielden, her lifelong friend, and is here shown on a cabinet photograph produced by C.F. Wiggins of Imperial Studio, Talbot Road, Blackpool in 1896. In later years she ran a small boarding house in Cleveleys, near Blackpool.

Central Station, 1905, after the rebuilding which began in 1899 and was completed for the Easter of 1901. The excursion platforms created at that busy time are gone, the area now serving mainly as a large car park.

The Winter Gardens, 1890. 'This noble pile of buildings is so easily discerned from any part of the town that it acts as a gigantic finger post.' This was pointed out in the earliest penny guide to Blackpool, printed by Abel Heywood shortly after the grand opening in 1878 by Sir Thomas Owden, Lord Mayor of London.

Steamers by the North Pier jetty taking on their loads of visitors in a good summer, *c.* 1900. From North and South piers, steamers continually plied to the Lake District, the Isle of Man and Liverpool, while sailing boats made pleasure trips within the bay. Cheap fares were part of Blackpool's recipe for success.

Talbot Road, 1880s. Dwelling houses with walled gardens were still to be seen instead of today's massed shops and wide pavements. T. Swarbrick's confectioner's shop is on the right; Henry Ibeson, hairdresser and perfumer, was at no. 42. Joseph Pickering and George Johnson had houses in Talbot Road at that time.

The Gigantic Wheel under construction, 1896. Set in 10 ft of concrete on columns, the axle alone weighed 30 tons. Its arrival was celebrated by a picture for the history books, showing workmen standing upon it and top-hatted councillors ranged below. The wheel, weighing 1,000 tons, rose 220 ft and each of its thirty carriages could hold thirty people.

Pleasure steamers at Blackpool, 1923. They gave a good view of a waterfront which became as famous as that of Liverpool. As the tide came in and crowds retreated to the wide promenade, the Tower, Gigantic Wheel and Palace were the popular alternatives.

A wagonette trip into the Blackpool countryside, *c.* 1900. Standing at the back is Miss Harrison of Raikes Parade. Wagonettes set off from Tyler's Boot Shop. This is one of the smaller conveyances but all gave a splendid view. Drivers were authorized to stop for visitors to buy Wardley's toffee, Hambleton 'hookings' (mussels) or teas at Mrs Simpson's in Over-Wyre.

Mr Wylie's Shard Hotel on the River Wyre before the first bridge opened in 1864. The novelty of being ferried across appealed to Blackpool visitors and there was good home-brewed ale at the inn. The lease of the Shard in 1908 contained a clause: 'An additional rental of £12 shall be charged whenever Shard Bridge is freed from toll.'

Foudroyant, Lord Nelson's flagship, wrecked at Blackpool on 16 June 1897. In 1895 it was on show at Blackpool after restoration and refitting, which cost £20,000. Anchored between Central and North piers, it broke moorings when a storm blew up, the weight of the three tiers of cannon contributing to its wrecking. Souvenirs were made from its timbers and copper. Two other ships were wrecked in salvage operations connected with the *Foudroyant*, but fortunately all the crew were rescued by lifeboat. There were a number of wrecks and disasters off the coast of Blackpool, including the burning of the *Ocean Monarch* which was caused by a passenger lighting a fire in a ventilator. Flames, which could be seen from Blackpool promenade, spread rapidly and the death toll was high. In August 1848 bodies from the *Ocean Monarch* were cast up at Blackpool.

Queen Square, North Shore, *c*. 1880. The Revd C.H. Wainwright was the incumbent of Christchurch, in the background. The area was given over to the three-storey houses of prosperous residents. Some became boarding houses, offering welcome accommodation for visitors.

These boarding houses in Queen Street, built in the nineteenth century, were all replaced with shops as the street became a fashionable centre for expensive clothes, furs and furniture. The lack of traffic except the handcart and landau suggests this is out-of-season in the 1880s.

Central Beach in the year when promenade-widening festivities were held, 1905. A great effort had been made to complete the work begun in 1902. New entrances for both North and Central piers further increased popularity so that by 1910 more extension was necessary.

South promenade from Manchester Hotel, c. 1902. This area had been transformed since the days of the 1833 storms when sandhills in front of Simpson's Hotel disappeared, along with cottages in Butcher's Row and Welsh's Row, a woodyard near Bennett's Hotel and the roofs of two newly built properties belonging to Mr E. Lewtas.

Our House Inn, Oddfellow Street, near Bonny Street. Rebuilt around the turn of the century, it boasted some fine engraved glass and ceramic tiles. The lamp, which would now be a collector's item, reflects the friendly atmosphere of a genuine old inn.

The original whitewashed Gynn Inn, the last of Blackpool's historic buildings, closed in May 1921 and was completely demolished after the contents had been auctioned. Residents and visitors mourned the passing of this famous landmark. The last of the Dreadnought trams, shown in this photograph, went for breaking up in 1935.

Boarding trams at South Shore, *c*. 1900. As with most Blackpool enterprises, the provision of trams was a huge success from the very start. The front tram, heading for the Manchester Hotel, displays the route: Blackpool, St Anne's, Lytham. They were also ideal vehicles for advertisements that provided extra revenue: Shinio, Wincarnis Wine, Gossage's Soap and A1 Sauce are seen here.

Track laying at South Shore, *c*. 1900. Seated on the bogie is head workman, Mr Garlick. The first electric trams in the country were operated by Blackpool Tramway Company in 1885 on a track 2 miles long. Gales and blowing sand were always a problem. In 1927, when the Fylde coast was flooded, a tram at North Shore was completely blown over.

The promenade, North Shore, early 1900s. This is a study in fashions of the day: white blouse, long skirt, boater, black umbrella to keep off the sun, toddler in frills and bonnet, and an old gentleman, seated, with the bushy white beard so favoured by elderly men of that time.

Claremont Park, c. 1904. Under an Act of Parliament in 1865 the Local Board borrowed £30,000 to construct a real promenade and extend the hulking. The Imperial Hotel had just been completed and the Claremont Park Estate was laid out in the same year.

The Prince of Wales Theatre became the site of the New Alhambra Theatre of Varieties, *c.* 1902. On the left is Herr Cohen's Health Depot. He held consultations daily, advising on fractious children and claimed to cure many ailments by using electricity.

Thought to be the old Grapes Inn run by John J. Brook, with the tin-plate worker Mr Wallworth next door, 1920s. Hanging on the left is probably the three-dimensional inn sign: bunches of grapes. Behind that on the left is Lloyds Bank.

HRH Princess Louise drew crowds when she opened the widened promenade in May 1912. North Pier's entrance had been set back, harmonizing with and enlarging the square where people gathered. An area of shops with onion-domed pavilions made for further enhancement. There was a great turnout of people to watch the procession of landaus from the station along the promenade. As special guests passed the North Pier in glorious weather, flags and bunting flew all over the town. Princess Louise's visit coincided with Blackpool's first attempt to illuminate the promenade. Ten thousand electric lamps were used to impress the Duke and Duchess of Argyll and the great crowds that assembled in Blackpool from far and wide. Alderman John Bickerstaffe received the honorary freedom of the borough together with Alderman J. Fish in 1912, and South Blackpool rejoiced in Waterloo Cinema.

The Cliffs, Blackpool, *c.* 1910. At this time they were partially protected by a sea wall. In the far distance is the Mount Hotel, advertising apartments for visitors. Crowds walking along the cliffs and sitting on the shore are obviously impressed by the extension of promenading facilities.

Hound Hill before Central station was altered, 1890s. The New Inn (rebuilt in 1896), Palatine Hotel and the Station Temperance Hotel were in this area. Signs of the times are the shoeblack boy (right) by the old pillar-box and the boy with the milk churn near the New Inn and Central Hotel.

The interior of the Alhambra Circus in the early years of this century, showing high wires, trapezes and rope ladders. The ornate ceiling and gilded boxes photographed by Rush and Warwick are echoed again in the next view. Blackpool's favourite circus clown was Charlie Cairoli, who reigned supreme for forty years.

The Grand Staircase from the Marble Hall, Alhambra, with its rich surroundings and huge bevelled mirrors impressed the crowds at the time of this publicity photograph, *c.* 1905. However, the Tower's four floors of entertainment with the lift ride to the top caused the Alhambra to become a loss-making enterprise.

Thompson's Railway, built by Mr W.G. Bean, showing the gypsy encampment in the background, 1907. So many people came to see both that timber railway sleepers had to be laid on the sands to form a causeway. The encampment moved in 1910 after complaints about sanitation.

Central Pier, 1906. North Pier had been such a success that Central Pier, originally called South Pier, seemed mandatory. Under the supervision of John Mawson, hired by Major Preston, it was opened on 30 May 1868 in readiness for the season, only one year after the first pile was driven.

The Empress Ballroom in the Winter Gardens was opened in 1896. Enterprising Manager Bill Holland had sensationally advertised the complex: 'Come to the Winter Gardens and spit on Bill Holland's 100 guinea carpet.' Visitors flocked in thousands, but they came to marvel and admire.

The Casino, Blackpool Pleasure Beach, 1933, a building with Monte Carlo in mind where working men could attempt to break the bank. This stylish architecture was replaced by a new casino in 1939, a year of vast building projects in Blackpool.

Paddling at South Shore early this century, a scene which fifty years earlier would have inspired letters to the newspaper, as at that time a section of the beach was set aside for ladies and girls. Even horses were thought to benefit from immersion in sea water, 'the universal panacea'.

Uncle Tom's Cabin, 1890. This had begun as a tiny enterprise forty years earlier when Margaret Parkinson opened a refreshment stall on Sundays from where she sold gingerbreads, nuts and home-made ginger beer. This was replaced by a wooden hut nicknamed Little London. The Parkinsons were then farming at Knowle near Beryl Hill.

The ballroom at the Alhambra. This fine building with its interiors created by craftsmen became the Palace after its purchase in 1903 by the Tower Company. The Empress Ballroom advertised on the Dreadnought trams had similar grand surroundings. Victoria Pier was a popular venue for Fylde farmers, well known from early days for their dancing prowess.

Central Pier, 'the pier for the masses', c. 1904. Eventually there were three piers. To ensure Blackpool's position as a first-class resort the corporation spent £1½ million in providing places of entertainment. Central Pier was a vantage point from which to view the Channel Fleet, anchored on 7 August 1907, and a Graf Zeppelin which passed over the town in 1932.

Embarking for the River Caves of the World, South Shore, *c.* 1906. 'Niagara' is in the background and to the right, the Switchback entrance. Under Mr Bean's direction, new rides and novelties were invented for each season. By the 1920s thrills were being provided by the new Velvet Coaster, so named because of the upholstery in the cars.

The Fair Ground, South Shore, built on the old gypsy encampment site amid the sandhills, 1910. The Scenic Railway, Helter Skelter and Mystic Circle were well patronized during Bank Holidays and Wakes Weeks. By 1927 there was a 'Kiddies' Amusement Park' where 250 prizes were offered in painting competitions, the entry fee being 3*d*.

The Palatine Family and Commercial Hotel, close to Central station and Central Beach, *c*. 1900. By 1889 under Tom Partington, the manager, it was well established as a family hotel. Blackpool catered for all types, with British Workman Rooms at South Shore. Auction and sale rooms were a feature of the town wherever crowds were thickest. Next to the Palatine, Craven's Sale Room was housed in the Royal Hotel where Miss Westaway was manageress. Auctioneer and salesman, Jabez S. Doidge, was a well-known character who set up in West Street in 1880. He died in 1928 at the age of ninety-three. In 1922 'Blackpool's popular auctioneer' was Percival Bailey who conducted auction sales twice a week in the Masonic Hall on Waterloo Road, South Shore, 'the largest and oldest-established auction rooms in Blackpool'.

Clifton Road thatched cottage, an example of a Fylde long house. Any building in the way of progress was rapidly swept away by order of the Corporation and very soon little of antiquity remained, yet strangely this thatched cottage persisted into the 1950s. The area of West Street where crowds remain thickest today, close to the Golden Mile and in the shadow of the Tower, still has Roberts' Oyster Rooms where oysters have been sold since 1876. In those days it was seven oysters for 1s and people were allowed to bring their own drink to wash the oysters down – 'black velvet', a blend of stout and champagne, being the most popular. Nowadays the oysters come from Ireland and Anglesey but the same family continues the business. In West Street are two original inns, the Fleece and the Mitre.

SECTION THREE

People and Events

Crowds on North Pier, *c.* 1902.

The Hippodrome in 1930 showed 'Living Pictures and Varieties'. It had opened as The Empire in 1895. The first cinema film show in Blackpool was in the Tower Ballroom, when John Bickerstaffe watched the *Queen of the North* steamboat amid a snowstorm of flickers on the silver screen.

'Progress 1885–1905' referred to this first electric tramcar, 'still running, which commenced running in September 1885'. Decked out at the tram sheds ready for parade in 1905, it made brave showing in a year full of progress: the promenade and cemetery were enlarged, there was motor racing in July, the new secondary school was built and Lytham Road bridge was rebuilt.

South Beach from Central Pier, 1880. The south end of Blackpool was developed later. A fine parade of boarding houses was built and smart, well-stocked shops like Tufnell and Thompson's were opened, complete with sun blinds. Rowing boats were available, and when the tide was out large, heavy carts carried visitors out to the waiting boats for sea trips. South Pier, originally the property of the Jetty Company Ltd, was built under the superintendence of the company's civil engineer, Colonel John Mawson. The first pile was driven on 3 July 1867. The 24 ft wide promenade decking stretched 1,000 ft. At the end of the pier an iron jetty 400 ft long was added. One of Blackpool's most popular summer attractions at that time was dancing on South Pier, where the platform was screened from winds by a framework of wood and glass. To promenade on the pier cost just 2d.

Laying the foundation stone for Blackpool Conservative Club alongside the Electric Baths, 1898. Mr A.J. Balfour performed the ceremony. The discovery of electricity led to its being applied therapeutically. Any new idea was grist to Blackpool's mill.

Central station's hoardings, before its first rebuilding which began in 1899, speak of early Blackpool attractions and commodities: Read's Seawater Swimming Baths, Keen's Mustard, the Aquarium, Aviary and Menagerie, the Winter Gardens, Samuel's watches and T. Simpson & Sons of Halifax. During Wakes Weeks this concourse was thronged.

The Winter Gardens, *c.* 1906. The Victoria Street entrance was used largely in summer as it communicated directly with the beach. Entering at the Church Street turnstile (6*d* in 1885), the visitor was immediately under the great dome, 120 ft high with a circumference of 126 ft. A large centrally placed bronze fountain and fish-pond was surrounded by twelve classical statues. The Floral Hall, full of rare plants and ferns, had refreshment stalls and news rooms. In the great Pavilion, which could seat 3,000 people, an orchestra played twice daily and from time to time all the leading singers appeared in concerts. Beneath the Pavilion were a grotto and stalactite cavern. The buildings, designed by Mr Mitchell of Manchester, were declared open in June 1878 by the Lord Mayor of London. They finally comprised the Empress Ballroom, Planet Room, Palm Café, Opera House, Pavilion Cinema, Renaissance Restaurant, Baronial Hall, Spanish Hall and the Olympia.

Central Beach, 1890. It still has gardens attached to premises, but signs of enterprise show in Sansome's Coffee Palace and Yorkman's Rooms with bath chairs and tricycles for hire. Cycles and mail carts could be hired from J. Collier along this stretch, now part of the Golden Mile.

Central Pier with tea and coffee bars to cater for the crowds, 1890. 'Read's Private Sea-Water Swimming and Plunge Baths' were prominently advertised on the kiosks, sea water being carted up daily. From the 400 ft long iron jetty, steamers and sailing boats added considerable interest to the scene.

Nicholson's Public Sea Water Baths were advertised in 1910 as the largest plunge in Blackpool, with Professor Faraday on hand to give lessons. He was reputed to be particularly skilful with nervous would-be swimmers. Blackpool was famous for its baths and both Read's and Nicholson's offered the buoyancy of sea water. At Read's over 100 gallons of sea water were pumped from the ocean into tanks and filtered. The Prince of Wales had sixty-one dressing rooms; towels, brushes, combs and costumes were supplied as well as 'lifebuoys for the nervous'. Turkish, Russian and Vapour baths were available at all establishments.

Largest Plunge in Blackpool.

Sea Water, Swimming, and Private Baths. Lessons by Prof. FARADAY.

LADIES: Tuesday and Thursday Afternoons.

FRED NICKSON, "STATION" HOTEL, TALBOT ROAD, BLACKPOOL.

SAVAGE SOUTH AFRICA

UNDER THE DIRECTION OF FRANK E. FILLIS & J. PITT HARDACRE.

Be Sure to Visit THE ELLIS FAMILY, PALMISTS & PHRENOLOGISTS

'Savage South Africa', one of Blackpool's most spectacular shows, under the direction of Frank E. Fillis and J. Pitt Hardacre, was staged in 1901 while the Boer War was being fought. The amazing array brought over from South Africa included: Lilian Revier – the champion lady rifle-shot of the Transvaal, the 6 ft 8 in tall Andries Ventor – a native of Pretoria who had fought against the Jameson Raiders before the Boer War, President Kruger's State Coachman, 100 Zulu, Basuto and Matabele natives, Texas Jack – a noted scout, the ox-wagon in which Mr Fillis lived for three months in South Africa, and so on. The Boer encampment, with genuine Transvaal Boers, was on view during the interval and the show, in four parts, reached its climax with the Battle of Elandslaagte, 'Britain v. Boer'.

The coronation of King George V and Queen Mary in 1911 was celebrated everywhere with great rejoicing. This gathering is on the sands at Blackpool. Children were given the 'freedom' of the town: free tram rides, a bonfire near Revoe, a gala and sports. Adults joined the ox-roasting event and firework displays.

''Pon my sole, Bispham suits me' is a postcard from the 1900s when the grassy cliffs, quieter than promenade or sands, made a pleasant retreat. Falls of the cliff face occurred until the 1950s, when paved walkways and cement secured them.

Blackpool donkey with Desmond astride against a backcloth of the Pleasure Beach, 25 July 1924. Donkeys on the sands wore their names on brass plates across their foreheads. The Donkeys' Charter prohibited heavy people from riding on these animals. Regulation 5 in 1942 at Blackpool stated: 'With reference to asses on the foreshore, no sticks or whips shall be used and the kicking of an ass is strictly prohibited.'

A First World War postcard sent to Mrs Yates of Blackpool from S 24 Army Post, passed by the censor, April 1918. Part of the message reads: 'I write this in the trench.' At Blackpool soldiers were prepared for the front in an area known as the Loos trenches, later shown to visitors on payment of a small fee.

The North Pier, an attraction for thousands of visitors with its many added improvements, 1913. The tramline, opened by the Mayor of Manchester in 1886, was a tremendous success. Crowds were brought in the thundering Dreadnought trams, one of which is shown in the foreground. The new promenade had been opened on Easter Monday, 18 April 1870, both promenade and pier being lit by electric light. 'The light is generated by nine of Siemens' dynamo electric machines, each nominally 6,000 candle power and requiring five indicated horse power to drive it. What Blackpool decides to do, it does well,' was the press report. One of the two pleasure boats *Wellington* and *Bickerstaffe* can be seen off the end of the pier. The best man to commission for the pier was undoubtedly Eugenius Birch, the Brunel of pier design in Queen Victoria's day, and Blackpool settled for no less. North Pier was where 'the better class of visitor' promenaded, but height of season photographs show it so crowded as years passed by that such niceties became anachronisms.

Opening of the Miners' Home, Bispham, by HRH the Prince of Wales, 28 June 1927. Later known as the Lancashire and Cheshire Mineworkers' Convalescent Home, the magnificent building had Jimmy Saville as guest at its sixtieth anniversary celebration.

King George V and Queen Mary were given a great welcome in Blackpool on 8 July 1913. Blackpool schoolchildren, the little girls all in white, lined the route. The town was smothered in flags and bunting with crowds everywhere.

The sensational and spectacular in the 1920s liven up a small section of the Golden Mile, so-called because of its money-making sideshows: Hilda Flack – the giant schoolgirl, the Ubangi savages, Ida Campbell – half woman, and Coney Island. The takings were collected in large zinc buckets. Jugs of tea were bought here to take on to the sands.

Soldiers' camp in the Fylde, possibly in the Blackpool area, *c.* 1912. The flat plain made it a good place for pitching tents in readiness for drill and firing practice every summer. The Blackpool Volunteer Artillery was founded in 1865. In its history Blackpool has played host to thousands of service men and women.

Landaus drawn up in 1907 at the new Uncle Tom's Cabin built on the east side of the tram track. The original cabin on the west side and the Gynn Inn had been subjected to the destructive forces of nature to such an extent that both had to be replaced. The *Blackpool Gazette* reported that the storm of 1875 had caused a dangerous cliff fall between the Gynn and Uncle Tom's Cabin. The Camera Obscura hut had been moved twice but the foundations were so undermined that it began to collapse. George Ashworth, licensee of Uncle Tom's Cabin since around 1900, closed it down in October 1907 and three months later the entire building was demolished. A 1911 survey showed that the sea took almost 8 ft of land every year. Earlier protection of the cliffs might have saved Uncle Tom's Cabin and the unusual mascots on the roof for posterity. The new hotel, if perhaps lacking the nostalgic appeal of the old, was more in tune with twentieth-century demands. Tea gardens and extra accommodation were added. To this day entertainment remains a feature, with traditional jazz provided every Wednesday night by the Festival Jazzmen.

C. Grahame-White at the Blackpool Flying Carnival. This second Blackpool flying meeting was held at Squire's Gate in 1910 when this intrepid aviator flew round the Tower and on to the Isle of Man. Some aircraft landed on the beach near South Shore. History was made when an aeroplane carried mail for the first time. The first Aviation Week was in 1909.

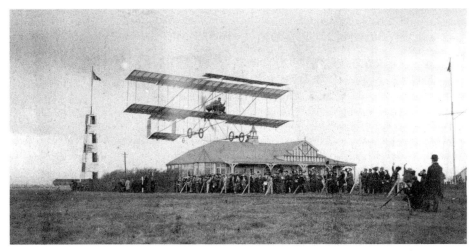

Aviation Week, 18–23 October 1909, at Blackpool. Although not the first in the country with Doncaster beating Blackpool by three days, it was the first official occasion, being sponsored by the Aero Club and with competitors and spectators insured. Immense crowds gathered from an early hour until 20,000 people were at the ground. Five British aviators competed: Singer, Roe, Charter, Mortimer and Neale.

Punch and Judy was a regular feature on Blackpool sands before the 1920s, along with ventriloquists, oyster and shrimp stalls, ice-cream vendors, rock sellers and quack doctors. Mr Toole, the Hair King, attracted huge crowds. This was in the days before the Corporation imposed controls and applications for licences.

Imperial Hotel and North Parade in the 1920s, when adults had less interest in the sands, preferring to walk the length of a fine promenade. In early days people were keen to drink sea water, which was medically approved. Blackpool Sea Water Company was registered in 1872 to supply sea water to houses and bottle it for health purposes. In 1922 four million tons of salt water were used to clean the streets.

The Della Rosa Band entertained at the Winter Gardens in 1900. Direct from Italy, it was its first appearance in England and the occasion was well advertised by the General Manager, J.R. Huddlestone. Appearing with them on the programme of 'extraordinary attractions' in the Victoria Annexe and Indian Lounge was the famous Imperial Tzigane Orchestra of Tota Nicolici.

Motor Trials at Blackpool involving speed trials on South Shore promenade were held in October 1904 and July 1905. Some of these cars may still chug along the promenade when the annual Veteran Car Rally assembles at Norbreck Castle Hydro.

Collinson's Café was well patronized by day-trippers in the 1920s. It was situated at North Shore above some interesting shops. Lyons were pianoforte dealers ('Feldman's songs and dances' is advertised on the sun blind). Shepherd & Company sold not only wines and spirits, but also patent medicines.

John Uttley & Sons Ltd, Furniture Removers of Blackpool in 1922, was even then an 'old firm'. Others were Donnelly's and Goulden's of Church Street – who supplied fashionable furs and ladies' clothing, Eastwood's – auctioneers of Birley Street, E. Coppock – newsagent – established 1894, and Henry Johns & Son – wine merchants – established 1864.

Blackpool Tower stands sentinel in 1929, a fine summer with crowds enjoying the beach and open-topped trams. Piles of deck-chairs are stacked ready for use. In this notable year the *West Lancashire Gazette* appeared for the first time, the Prince of Wales, Prince Paul of Greece and Prime Minister Stanley Baldwin visited the resort, and the Hippodrome and Princess Cinemas were sold. Visitors to the Tower Buildings learned that five million bricks went into its construction. In the Tower itself engineers used 2,493 tons of steel and 93 tons of cast iron. At a time of industrial depression, Blackpool remained so popular that John Heeson made a model of the Tower from 55,000 spent matches, which took him 7½ years. Twenty specialized men have always worked to preserve the Tower; riggers, painters and builders use rigs identical to those when the Tower was built in 1894. Poles are specially imported from Norway, seasoned to prevent rot and renewed after only four years. A Memory Lane Show in the Tower displays a 3 ft spanner from 1893.

The wooden bridge at Bispham connecting part of the cliffs above the slope and the series of wooden hand bridges leading down to the shore, 1900. Since then many changes have taken place. The rural aspect of the village was eventually to disappear completely with the cliffs shrouded in concrete.

A landlady with a group outside a Blackpool boarding house, 1920s. Visitors could bring their own food to be cooked and were usually 'charged for the cruet'. Itinerant photographers went from street to street capturing such groups. In 1922 the Blackpool Company of House Proprietors decided to retain their charge of 4s per bed per night.

Talbot Road station, photographed shortly before it was rebuilt in 1896. The new station opened in 1898. A notice points to the excursion platforms. Holiday-makers with luggage were conveyed by horse and cart and landau rather than by taxi. Blackpool's publicity manager, Mr Naden, acted instantly with countrywide telegrams whenever major events such as pier openings and the wrecking of the *Foudroyant* occurred, and the railway company responded with extra trains.

A group of newspaper reporters on a Central station platform, *c.* 1920. The *Blackpool Times* was started in 1877 with two local ministers as joint editors: the Revd J. Wayman, Congregational, and the Revd Samuel Pilling, Baptist. The first edition of the *Blackpool Gazette*, published by John Grime at the Steam Printing Works, Church Street, appeared on 3 April 1873, price 1*d*.

Blackpool Beach in front of the Tower with visitors amusing themselves, 1920s. It was here that my little sister got lost. A tall man in the throng paraded Sheila on his shoulders, and she was soon returned to the bosom of her family and her distraught mother. At an early stage the Blackpool pioneers recognized two types of visitor: the day excursionist and the week-long holiday-maker. While the health-giving breezes and close proximity of Tower to beach were ideal, these needed to be supplemented by more entertainment. They ventured upon projects which became the envy of other seaside resorts. Among the earliest were the Crystal Palace, Alpine Hall and Uncle Tom's Cabin. Both Belle Vue and Strawberry Gardens near Whitegate Drive offered dancing and pretty scenery but prospered for only a while as did their imitator, Raikes Hall, owing to their distance from the sea.

Smiling trippers coming off excursion train no. 91 in the early 1900s. Factories like Bury Felt brought in their entire workforce on no. C 871 for coronation celebrations on 1 June 1953. Lancashire Wakes Weeks saw similar crowds and at the end of the week it was back home to Preston, Rochdale, Oldham and Manchester, all spent up. Only the railway could cater effectively for these huge crowds visiting Blackpool annually. In August 1933 the LMS Railway Company conveyed and brought back half a million passengers, figures which were repeated during the autumn illuminations. Return holiday tickets available for seventeen days on any day of the week by any train cost only the price of the ordinary single fare, plus one-third. 'Runabout' tickets offered unlimited travel for a week anywhere within a large radius for 10s. Throughout the season all-in tickets included the fare, a meal and a show. No wonder people came again and again!

Councillor H. Brooks, Blackpool's mayor 1922–3, first visited the town in 1881 when he was a circus performer, already having established a reputation as a gymnast on the continent. After an accident in March 1887 Mr Brooks gave up circus life and settled in Blackpool with his wife to run the Adelphi Hotel on Church Street. By 1897 he had been appointed managing director of the Alhambra on the promenade, which later became the Palace. Energetic in politics and charity work, he was also associated with Blackpool's Royal Antediluvian Order of Buffaloes. He attended the ceremony in the Tower Pavilion when Mr Lloyd George was presented with the honorary Freedom of the Borough.

A charabanc trip from Poulton to Blackpool, 1923. Billy Yates, whose father was a Blackpool resident, is the small boy near the front; behind him is his grandmother, Lucy Lang. They lived at Lower Green, having moved from Church Street where Billy was born.

The Wright family of Blackpool, later of Fleetwood, 1914. Back row, left to right: Jenny, John, Richard, Molly (a companion. Front row: Mary Alice, Emily Annie (born 1899), Richard (skipper of a prawner). Mary Alice was in service in Blackpool when she met and married Richard. A son, James Poole, became chief engineer on the steam trawler *Queen Alexandra*.

The Dodgem, the first in Europe, *c.* 1900. This was part of W.G. Bean's idea of creating an American-style amusement park at Blackpool's South Shore. He laid down the Hotchkiss Patent Bicycle Railway in 1896 and erected the Helter-Skelter Slide and the Sir Hiram Maxim's Captive Flying Machine. With the River Caves in 1906 Mr Bean had achieved his purpose but his heirs have continued the tradition and eventually have outdone the USA with the present-day Roller Coaster, the highest and fastest in the world. Mr Bean, who founded the Pleasure Beach Company in 1910, was a shrewd businessman who foresaw great possibilities in exploiting the Starr Hills. He became a respected alderman, and was listed with others in the borough (Cardwell, Potter, Lumb, Nickson and Ward) in a report dated 7 January 1933 as 'giants of their time who pointed Blackpool in the right direction'.

Crowds flock past the beautiful Casino, a building reminiscent of the Venetian Doges Palace, 1925. The Seven Orpheians played here and dancing was on offer each afternoon. Both a restaurant and a popular café were open to the public. The Reel pleasure ride can be seen on the right.

The Reel, a Blackpool Pleasure Beach favourite ride during the 1923 season. Under 'Mind Your Hats' the small print warns that the management takes no responsibility. This did not deter the crowds who flocked to pay the 6d fare.

The 17th Earl of Derby KG, present at many important Blackpool occasions, opened Stanley Park in 1925. The making of this extensive park near Victoria Hospital, 250 acres of land costing 4½d a square yard, provided work for hundreds of unemployed men. Two years later the Stanley Park Cocker Memorial Clock Tower, in memory of William H. Cocker, was opened by Alderman Sir John Bickerstaffe.

Mr Rowland Hill, Chief Librarian at the time of Blackpool's Jubilee Year in 1926, suggested a brochure, *Blackpool's Progress*, to celebrate the occasion. This would exploit the pictorial section of its Carnegie Library to show 'the remarkable and unexampled popularity of Blackpool as the finest and greatest health resort in the United Kingdom'. Copies of some of the prints are included in this book.

Excursion platforms at Central station, 1920. As many as fifty locomotives were kept at the Blackpool sheds to cope with all the excursion trains. In August 1941 a crowded train had just left Central station when part of a plane crashed down after a collision.

Fir Grove, under construction, 1933–4, looking south towards Glastonbury Avenue (left), Mayfair Road and Laurel Avenue, the area off Waterloo Road near Marton Library. At this time Charles Harding & Sons were selling freehold houses for £495. The model Bee Bee biscuit factory in Devonshire Road was also being built.

Blackpool North Pier fire, 11 September 1921. All the instruments of the North Pier Orchestra were destroyed when the Pavilion was burned down. On 6 January the Instruments Replacement Fund closed at £534. North Pier Pavilion was burned out for the second time on 19 June 1938 but repair quickly followed as 'walking over the water' never lost its appeal.

The North Pier Pavilion on fire, 19 June 1938. Damage amounted to £30,000. Over 200,000 holiday-makers watched columns of fire and smoke from the blazing structure rise to a height of hundreds of feet. Refurbishment began as soon as possible.

The Italian Gardens at Stanley Park, late 1930s. Italian statues were placed in the proximity of the lily pond, which looked splendid when the tiered fountain played. The two lions with the balls were authentic replicas of those in Florence.

The Colonnade and Rockery, North Shore, in the 1930s, illustrating how building along 'the seven golden miles' reflected confidence and stability. By this time Blackpool was the foremost resort in the country, offering more than anywhere else.

The Open Air Baths, South Shore, 1937. Crowds indicate the prevalence of a good summer and a popular venue while styles in bathing-costumes make the period unmistakable. On South Pier the Arcadian Follies was a show running all summer while on North Pier Lawrence Wright's *On With the Show* had appeared annually since 1924. South Shore Marine Baths opened in 1923 together with other South Shore extensions. Sketch plans were published in the *Gazette* and *Herald* in February 1922. On the south promenade from the Manchester Hotel much building had taken place. 'How the shrewd pioneers ensured £350,000 for the town in thirty years of rapid progress' was the theme of Charles Furness's article when Jubilee year, 1926, came round. 'Blackpool', said this engineer, 'owns a gold mine.'

Boarding Houses in Rigby Road near the promenade and Manchester Square, 1930s. At the end of the street is the imitation windmill which covered the old red-brick conveniences. Repairs are in progress for a new holiday season.

The Pleasure Beach on Whit Monday, 12 May 1913, with the traditional turnout of huge crowds from Lancashire and Yorkshire mill towns. A rock stall on the right is doing good business. 'Bobbing up and down like this' reads the notice under The Great American Dodgers stall, 'three balls for a shilling.'

Gracie Fields, the great-hearted, talented 'Lancashire lass' who never forgot her roots, was a friend to Blackpool. Here she starred in a film about the town, *Sing As We Go*. Through her generosity hundreds of deprived sick children came to benefit from the wonderful sea air. Her Cinderella Home for children became Rossall Hospital. Blackpool was also a favourite place to perform for George Formby, in whose memory the George Formby Society meets annually. Some members who joined at age seven are now seventy.

Walter Howarth's original programme for the performance of *The Prisoner of Zenda* on Monday 13 February 1899 at the Grand Theatre and Opera House, Blackpool. Walter was a regular theatre-goer who lived in St Anne's-on-Sea. Thomas Sergenson, the manager, who came to Blackpool in 1876, was connected with the Prince of Wales Theatre upon which he took a five-year lease as he did for the Theatre Royal (later the Tivoli Cinema), but his dream was to build the Grand Theatre for which he commissioned Frank Matcham. To this end he purchased a good site on Church Street. 'Matcham's Masterpiece' or 'the prettiest theatre in the Kingdom' continues today, beautifully gilded and restored by the Friends of the Grand.

The Blackpool Illuminations of 1927 in Talbot Square, with part of a tableau depicting the seasons. An illuminated tramcar gliding along the front at nightfall made an eye-catching spectacle, a feature continued to this day. Over the years on Blackpool Tower alone, 10,000 lamps have had to be maintained throughout the illuminations. Celebrities ranging from Jayne Mansfield to Red Rum have switched on Blackpool's lights.

The Model Yacht Pond on the south promenade, 1931. Its massive pillars topped with classical urns make a striking postcard. The tram track runs on the left. 'Having a great time, weather splendid,' writes a Scottish visitor, one of thousands from that part of Great Britain who continue to rate Blackpool highly.

The ever-popular Scenic Railway, 1900s. In 1934 a fire on the Pleasure Beach destroyed the Chinese Theatre and Miniature Railway. There was further tragedy in 1938 when the casino floor collapsed while under construction, killing four men and injuring two. In 1939 there was yet another fire.

Staff of Highfield School, Blackpool, c. 1946. Back row, left to right: a student, J. Wood, C. Stockton, N. Bell, H. Makin, W. Naylor, M. Bollington, W. Yates, J. Sanderson, R. Breeze. Front row: N. Bates, H. Coupy, T. Dixon, V. McKenna, G. Ford (headmaster), H. Pearson (deputy head), T. Mayhew, E. Marsh, D. Shorrocks.

A postcard of a rough sea at Blackpool, June 1947. In the June of thirty years before, visitors wrote: 'Had a sail to Morecambe today and it was grand.' These sea trips being no more in the 1940s, Fred writes: 'Could you send some cigs?'

A great snowfall in the winter of 1940 almost submerged the colonnades at Highfield School. Blackpool schools closed and transport was temporarily halted. In wartime the town became a reception area for service men and accommodated 100,000 evacuees and expectant mothers. Civil servants were sent from London with vital records to be housed in the hotels.

SECTION FOUR
Time Marches On

Blackpool traffic wardens introduced in 1961, headed by J. Dobson (left) and P.K. Kenniford.

These crowds on the promenade and beach in 1931 still came to see Blackpool Tower, 'the magnet' or 'red pepper shaker'. When Gustave Eiffel constructed his famous tower for the Paris Exhibition of 1889 the London-based Standard Contract & Debenture Corporation planned to erect similar towers in seaside resorts throughout Britain. Only New Brighton and Blackpool achieved this and only Blackpool's has survived. Throughout the year, as soon as painters reach the bottom, up they go again to start repainting. Eric Redfern, Tower engineer, reports that each coat takes 4 tons of red lead and 1½ tons of red oxide paint and constant painting has given the Tower a coat 1 in thick. Only 75 m.p.h. winter gales, which give the Tower a 1 in sway, stop the work. In its centenary year, 1994, it has been painted gold.

In 1930 the Palace had a ballroom, an Italian lounge and three superb pleasure pavilions with variety acts and films. It offered 'the entertainment experience of a lifetime'. Billy Cotton and his Band were then playing. The Palace began as the Blackpool Alhambra, the foundation stone being laid on 4 December 1897 by George R. Sims, then a well-known playwright. Purchased by the Tower Company, it reopened as the Palace on 4 July 1904. The Palace Theatre of Varieties could seat 2,800. Pulled down to make way for a large Lewis's store, that too has been partially phased out in fast-moving Blackpool. By 1933 Blackpool's 'super theatres' were the Hippodrome and Princess, offering three hours of entertainment with double-feature programmes of stars of the silver screen: John Barrymore, Jack Hulbert, Charles Laughton and Tallulah Bankhead.

Riley & Sons' milliner's and outfitter's shop in Corporation Street was pulled down in 1936 after a fire on 7 October of that year, which burned down the municipal offices and Messrs Boots, chemists, in two hours. Fire brigades from Blackpool, Fleetwood and Lytham attended. Fireman Raymond Laycock was killed. Town Hall office boys dragged out whatever records could be saved until heat and the imminent danger of floor collapse forced them to withdraw. Riley's had to sell off remaining fire-damaged stock after being in business since 1871.

Blackpool Beach in the summer of 1934, reflecting the popularity of Britain's foremost seaside resort which over the past 150 years had built up a reputation for world-class entertainment, spectacle and value for money. The last of the bathing machines, crowded together, are still used for changing. The sea is alive with bathers and on the shore folk can hardly move. Pleasure boats fill up as the patient horse harnessed to the heavy cart is prepared to take visitors to the boats. The Tower dominates a promenade thick with pedestrians and North Pier beckons. Success is written everywhere. In the 1930s Blackpool blossomed further as a conference town. Thirty organizations met in 1932 including all three political parties (Conservative, Labour and Liberal); the Free Church Council; the Refuge and the Prudential Assurance Companies; United Textile Factory Workers' Association, Dyers, Bleachers and Finishers, and Operative Bakers. Unsurpassed in provision of suitable conference halls, excellent accommodation, entertainment and geographical position, Blackpool provided for the whole of the British Isles.

Jackson Brothers, Automobile Engineers of Abingdon Street, Blackpool advertised this 'up to date 20 h.p. four cylinder car' along with others, *c.* 1916. Cars could be hired for long or short runs by telephoning Blackpool no. 69. Williams Bros on Whitegate Drive advertised Armstrong Siddeley 12 h.p. saloons with the famous self-changing gear from £265. The fingerpost points to Poulton and Singleton.

The 'toast-rack' circular tram ride of the 1920s, costing 6*d*, followed a route from Talbot Square along Abingdon Street, Church Street to Oxford and Waterloo Road, Lytham Road and back. On Whitegate Drive trams passed The Elms which became Elmslie School. By 1932 C. Smith's Coaches leaving Vance Road at 8 a.m. went daily to London, return fare 25*s*.

The Carnegie Library, opened by Lord Shuttleworth on 26 October 1911.

Christ Church, Queen Street, 1980s. Today a job centre covers the site.

Blackpool Town Hall, *c.* 1960. Originally it had a spire with a weather-vane on top in the form of a scale-model ship 7 ft high and 6 ft long. Hull, beam, bowsprit, rudder and mainsail were all authentic. In later years the spire became unsafe and had to be removed. Blackpool, constituted a county borough in 1904, had 32,000 local government electors by 1922, as against 1,713 burgesses in 1876.

Raikes Hall Hotel, 1970s. The Raikes Hall Park Gardens and Aquarium were formed a hundred years earlier and were favourites until supplanted by the Winter Gardens. A guest at the Niagara Building (which later became the Colosseum, Blackpool's first cinema), was Blondin, who crossed Niagara Falls by tightrope.

Since 1844 there have been markets on the site shown in this 1930s view. In St John's off Lytham Street, alongside stalls piled high with fruit, vegetables and cheeses, was 'everything to suit the tastes of souvenir seekers'. Waterloo Market sold toys, presents, drapery, picture postcards, novelties and had Penny Stalls (nothing over 1*d*). (Courtesy *Evening Gazette*.)

Central station excursion platforms with crowds waiting to board the 'specials' for Preston and beyond, 18 August 1917. These trains would use the third or 'new' line and after passing through Blackpool South with a full load would find it a hard pull to the bridge over Hawes Side Lane. At peak departure time there would be only a matter of minutes between trains.

The American Dodgem on the Pleasure Beach, which was billied as Blackpool's premier outdoor attraction, 'the acme aggregation of varied entertainment', c. 1910. The Great Spectatorium, the first in Europe, depicted the Battle of the Monitor and Merrimac. There was also the unique Velvet Coaster, the biggest skating rink, the Canadian Water Chute, the Scenic Railway, the Weird Katzenjammer Castle, the romantic River Caves and the exhilarating Canadian Toboggan.

Blackpool beach, 1977. Windbreaks had been invented, the bucket and spade era was dying out, fewer donkeys were available but children still loved to see them arrive each morning, walking daintily down the slades, with bells jingling. The donkeys spend their winters in Fylde pastures. 'Oyster Bill's' stall, a favourite in 1932, and others were replaced by motorized vehicles.

Church Street looking towards St John's Church, 1930s. Shops and other premises came and went during the early years of the twentieth century. The News Theatre, the Tatler along with Jackson's Tailors, Southworth's butchers and the pie shop on the left disappeared and the area became pedestrianized in the 1980s. In 1910 the thrifty went to Dawson's Divi Stores in Church Street, where they had five adjacent premises and paid a dividend at the rate of 1½*d* in the shilling. St John's Church on the site of the old 1821 church, almost unchanged since its rebuilding in 1878, was designed by Messrs Garlick, Park and Sykes, the cost of its erection being £12,000. The tower, 139 ft high, contains a peal of eight bells. (Courtesy *Evening Gazette*.)

Queen Elizabeth II and the Duke of Edinburgh attending the Royal Variety Show at the Opera House, 1955. Jack Hylton introduced the Queen to the world-famous clown of Blackpool Tower Circus, Charlie Cairoli. The royal train was kept at Poulton-le-Fylde in a quiet siding, but local residents saw the Queen glittering and magnificent in jewels and long gown when the royal party returned to the train for the night. The Queen and the Duke of Edinburgh visited again for Blackpool Tower's 100th anniversary in July 1994, when the Queen was presented with a 3ft stick of rock. (Courtesy *Evening Gazette*.)

Thomas Bickerstaffe JP was Blackpool's Jubilee Mayor in 1926. One of the Bickerstaffe brothers, he did much to promote Blackpool's fame, as did John S. Brodie, Borough Surveyor, who advised the Corporation to increase the promenade widening to 100 ft, which is still adequate today. At the opening ceremony 200 carriages carried civic leaders from dozens of towns and cities; streets were decorated, buildings floodlit and a banquet laid on for five hundred people.

'Mr Blackpool' (Reginald Dixon) standing by his mighty Wurlitzer organ. Blackpool, one of the greatest entertainment centres on earth, played host to countless personalities, but Reginald Dixon was a popular fixture for years with his bright and breezy signature tune 'I do like to be beside the seaside'. He lived in nearby Poulton, on Blackpool Old Road. The Wurlitzer, installed in the Tower Ballroom in 1935, was familiar to thousands. Considered the greatest instrument of its kind in Europe, it came from Illinois; the 150 stops were made to Reginald Dixon's specifications. In the winter of 1977 it was overhauled by organ specialist J.W. Walker of Suffolk at a cost of £50,000.

Members of the St Mark's Men's Fellowship breaking up one of the last of the thirty coaches of the Gigantic Wheel on 20 May 1954, having no further use for it as a meeting place. When the carriages were sold by public auction on 29 October 1928 they were taken to different parts of the country for a variety of uses, from hen cabins to society headquarters. The last remaining one is thought to be part of the Big Wheel Café at Over-Wyre. (Courtesy *Evening Gazette*.)

Frankie Vaughan (in foreground), appearing at Blackpool in the show bearing his name, opened the Blackpool Boys' Club Building Fund at a Garden Party held at St George's School, Marton, on 24 July 1961. Along with many other show personalities present, he signed autograph books. Among the many stars who performed in Blackpool were Marlene Dietrich, Gracie Fields, Diana Dors, Googie Withers, George Formby, Jon Pertwee and Morecambe and Wise. (Courtesy *Evening Gazette*.)

The film *The First Auto* was shown at the Winter Gardens Pavilion, and to underline the event this 1903 Buick car was lent by Premier Garages, South Shore, once a livery stable. 'This product of General Motors,' reads the notice, 'manufacturers of Buick cars.' An interested crowd gathered for instruction. It was fitted with a large bicycle bell that sounded like a fire alarm. (Courtesy *Evening Gazette*.)

Alderman J.R. Quayle stands outside Blackpool Town Hall with civic heads and Amy Johnson (far right) in the 1930s. The pioneer woman aviator had given a lecture after her epic flight to Australia on 27 September 1931. This deed so caught the public's imagination that a catchy song, 'Amy, wonderful Amy', was composed. Her husband and fellow-aviator, Jim Mollison, also came to Blackpool in January 1933. Jack Quayle was in the tradition of councillors who, like Dr Cocker, believed in inviting personalities to build up Blackpool's fame regardless of expense. Lillie Langtry, Sir Harry Lauder, Vesta Tilley, Sir Alan Cobham, Vivien Leigh, Winston Churchill, Gertrude Lawrence and Rafael Kubelik are but a few in the long list of notables from all walks of life who visited the town. In order to persuade Blériot, the pioneer French air ace, to visit it is said that golden guineas were heaped on the table of the Council Chamber. (Courtesy *Evening Gazette*.)

Marching workers with their wives on the promenade in March 1957 protesting against the threatened closure of the Hawker Aircraft factory. They were on their way to a mass meeting at the Winter Gardens Pavilion to call on the Government to save their jobs. Thousands had been left jobless by the closing of this factory at Squire's Gate in 1948. Hawker Aircraft had taken the vacant Squire's Gate factory in 1951 to build Hunter jets. Hawker Hunters were in production in 1954 at Squire's Gate but in 1955 the workers staged a ten-week strike. 1954 was a historic year. Princess Margaret visited Hawker Hunter's factory, the Princess Royal (Mary) opened Arnold Girls' School, Lord Martonmere (Mr J.R. Robinson) was knighted, the trawler *Evelyn Rose* was lost at sea and Lytham Boat Yard launched its last vessel, *The Drake*. (Courtesy *Evening Gazette*.)

Seaside rock makers in a Blackpool factory, 1938. Gentle rolling of the rock required four assistants and a supervisor. The inscription 'Blackpool Rock' lasted all the way through to the last suck. Other traditional sweetmeats were large humbugs. Trippers gathered round to see the rock made and one busker on the sands in the 1930s drew attention by throwing sticks of rock into the crowd.

Douglas Bickerstaffe JP, Chairman of Blackpool Tower and Winter Gardens Companies, with some of the principal dancers of the Children's Ballet at their end of season party, 1972. Inaugurated by Bill Holland, this annual feature at the Tower ran for sixty years. From the left: Betty Clarkson, Betty Davies, Marie Brown, Mr Bickerstaffe, Maureen Wilson, June Naden. (Courtesy *Evening Gazette*.)

Layton station with Crossley's, timber merchants, to the right, 1962. This was the first railway route to Blackpool when the Preston & Wyre Railway opened a branch line from Poulton in 1847. In spite of the Depression the LMS Railway carried half a million passengers to Blackpool in 1933. Trains arrived at fifteen-minute intervals, each carrying around eight hundred travellers.

This 200-year-old building, The Cottage, on the corner of Newhouse Road was so famed for its fish and chips in the 1970s that American visitors came to taste this traditional Lancashire meal. Originally Flag Causeway Farm, where the Johnsons lived, by the 1900s Mrs Quinn made fish and chips for sale, so starting the tradition.

The popular children's boating pool, North Shore, and the new lift to the top of the cliffs, 1960s. The site had originally been considered for open-air baths. This view shows how secure the cliffs had been made. The lift is no longer in service and the paddle-boats, which more than once were washed out to sea in rough winters, were gone by the 1940s.

The Derby Baths in 1978 before deterioration and declining patronage led to its demolition in the 1980s. This Olympic-standard swimming pool was officially opened by Lord Derby on 10 November 1965, although the main block was completed before the Second World War. H. Joyce & Sons were the builders and contractors.

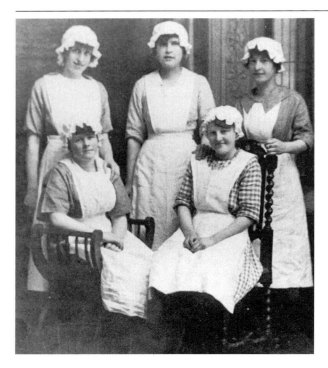

Edie and Maggie Cardwell (front) are in this group of girls, all of whom worked at the Parkhurst Bakery, Blackpool, in the 1930s. Girls who had hitherto worked only on farms found employment in Blackpool as it grew in popularity year by year. Edie and Maggie were happy with Sunday School and a charabanc outing each year. Their mother baked all the bread for the family, who lived in Carleton but had Cardwell relatives in Blackpool.

Stella, Paul and John Rothwell with Father Christmas at the Co-op Emporium, Blackpool, in 1962. The growth of the Blackpool Co-operative Wholesale Society proved consistent with that of the borough. A few railway workers discussed the possibility in their hut one lunchtime, resulting in a meeting in March 1885 held in Clarke's Coffee Palace. The first shop opened was in Lytham Street, now Corporation Street, and Blackpool soon realized the benefit of co-operative trading. In 1932 sales exceeded £900,000 and dividend paid £94,000. Valuable education programmes were organized by the CWS and there was a flourishing Co-operative Choral Society in Blackpool.

The Tower, viewed from North Pier in the summer of 1977, the year of the Queen's Silver Jubilee. There are still donkeys on the sands but motor vehicles have replaced the stalls. The new Lewis's building, which offers magnificent views from its Ward Room Restaurant, is to the left of the Tower. Such a classical example of Victorian architecture, Blackpool Tower was declared a Grade 2 listed building on 10 October 1973. After the magnificent ornate restoration of the world-famous Tower Ballroom, destroyed by fire in 1956, the Department of the Environment will possibly reassess and grade it to national category. 'The Wonderland of the World' was boldly lettered at the foot of Blackpool Tower in 1923 and this belief continues. Lord Delfont of New First Leisure Corporation bought the Blackpool Tower complex with other leisure and entertainment properties in a £37½ million deal from Lord Forte of Trust House Forte. The refurbished North Pier was reopened by Lord Delfont in July 1991.

Acknowledgements

Max Armstrong • *Blackpool Evening Gazette* • Blackpool Library
Blackpool Pleasure Beach • James Burkitt • Stanley Butterworth
Mrs F. Clegg • The Courtauld Institute • Mrs Cowperthwaite
Norman Cunliffe • Colin Dennison • First Leisure Corporation • J.J. Fish
John Gowland • Mrs Ibberson • Lancashire Library
Lancashire Record Office • Barry McLoughlin • John McGlynn
Harold Monks • Nostalgia Postcard Collectors' Club
Leah and Sarah Petulengro • Mr and Mrs Richard Poole
Red Rose Postcard Club • Ron Severs • Ralph Smedley • Bill Yates